Reading and Writing for
Urban Survival

First Edition, First Printing

Copyright 2016 by Jawanza Kunjufu

(Kiswahili for dependable and cheerful)

10-Digit ISBN #: 0-910030-19-7

13-Digit ISBN #: 978-0-910030-19-9

We recommend classroom use.

Volume discounts are available.

Visit our web site at

http://www.AfricanAmericanImages.com

or

e-mail us at

Customersvc@AfricanAmericanImages.com

African American Images

Chicago, Illinois

Preface

First, I think you are brilliant and extremely intelligent. I have listened to you. You have told me you are bored. You want books about your community and culture. I have heard you numerous times ask your teacher, "Why do we have to learn this?" I also know some of you have never read a book that you could not stop reading. You have only read books required to earn a grade. You asked for this book and I have tried to give you everything you asked. I would love to hear from you. I just have one more request. I want you to use your life to make a difference.

Your older brother,
Dr. Jawanza Kunjufu.

The Last Wish

A death row inmate awaiting execution, asked as a last wish a pencil and paper. After writing for several minutes, the convict called the prison guard and asked that this letter be handed over to his biological mother.

The letter said ...

Mother, if there were more justice in this world, we would be both executed and not just me. You're as guilty as I am for the life I led.

Remind yourself when I stole and brought home the bicycle of a boy like me? You helped me to hide the bicycle so my father would not see it. Do you remember the time I stole money from the neighbor's wallet?

You went with me to the mall to spend it.

"READING" for Urban Survival

Do you remember when I argued with my father and he's gone?

He just wanted to correct me because I stole the final result of the competition and for that I had been expelled.

Mom, I was just a child, shortly after I became a troubled teenager and now I'm a pretty malformed man.

Mom, I was just a child in need of correction, and not an approval. But I forgive you!

I just want this letter to reach the greatest number of parents in the world, so they can know what makes all people, good or bad ...is education. Thank you mother for giving me life and also helping me to lose it.

Your child offender.

What are your thoughts?

"WRITING" for Urban Survival

What do you think about the most?

What bothers you the most?

"READING" for Urban Survival

What makes you feel good?

How can we eliminate police brutality?

How can we increase jobs in the community?

Is the drug dealer the only one hiring in the Black

community?

"READING" for Urban Survival

How can we reduce violence?

What are your views on gangs in your community?

How would you negotiate a truce among rival gangs?

"WRITING" for Urban Survival

Do you buy hot goods? Why?

Would you buy your stolen flat screen back?

What are your thoughts on the "n" word?

What is the difference between nigger, nigga and niggaz?

If nigga means a term of endearment try using it with your parents and grandparents.

Gill Scott Heron one of the original rappers said to the new rappers is she a "b" or a queen? You can't call her a "b" on one song and a queen on the other unless you are bi-polar.

Should we legalize marijuana, heroin or cocaine?

Where in your neighborhood can you buy a gun?

Can you buy guns and drugs at school?

Do liquor stores sell to minors?

Where are the crack houses?

"READING" for Urban Survival

What is the criminal disparity between crack and cocaine? Why?

Is there a war on drugs or a war on Black and Hispanic men?

"WRITING" for Urban Survival

What percent of drug users are Black?

What percent of Blacks are convicted for drug

possession?

What percent of drug users are White?

What percent of Whites are convicted for drug possession?

What is driving while Black?

What is walking while Black?

What is shopping while Black?

What is standing on the corner

while Black?

"WRITING" for Urban Survival

What are the most frequent types of businesses in the Black community? Why?

Would you rather work a minimum wage job or sell drugs?

Why do Blacks get so many parking and driving tickets?

"READING" for Urban Survival

How many Blacks kill each other?

How many Blacks were killed last year by the police?

Do we place more responsibility on the police when they kill Blacks or when Blacks kill each other?

Do you know someone who was killed? Write them a letter. Do you know someone Black in jail? Write them a letter.

"WRITING" for Urban Survival

Do you know someone who was shot and is now paralyzed? Write them a letter.

What are your 5 favorite video games?

Describe riding on public transportation. Are elders respected in your neighborhood? Should elders reprimand youth?

Why do designer gym shoes sell so high if they are made overseas for less than $3.00?

How much would you pay for Nike Air Jordan? Would you pay $1000? Would you camp out for days in front of a store to be the first to own a new pair? Would you beat someone for their Jordans?

What are your chances of going pro in the NBA or WNBA? What are your chances of getting a rap contract? What are your chances of becoming a drug dealer and never caught?

What are your recreation options on evenings and weekends?

How do you feel about religion and church?

"WRITING" for Urban Survival

If you were school principal what changes would you make?

How would you reduce the dropout rate?

Suspension? Special education placement?

How would you increase test scores? Attendance?

A Black male was the valedictorian of his class. He wore a beard the entire school year. He was told on graduation day at the school unless he shaved he could not participate. He chose not to shave. Your thoughts?

How did Asians and Nigerians outscore Whites on the SAT if the tests are culturally bias? What will you score on the SAT? What is your GPA? Do you have good study habits? Describe.

What is the schoolhouse to jailhouse pipeline?

Does your school look like a prison?

What does it mean orange is the new black? Why do 2 million students have police officers in their schools, but no counselors? A 5-year-old female student was acting up in the school. The teacher called the principal, who called the police. The girl was placed in the police car by herself, driven to the police station and was locked up until her parents arrived. Your thoughts? How do females feel when security guards inspect their purse and their sanitary napkins and other personal items?

How would you make it look like a school?

Are schools designed to educate everyone or to

educate only those in magnet, honors and gifted?

If you were the mayor what would you do

differently?

If you were the governor what would you do

differently?

"WRITING" for Urban Survival

If you were the president what would you do differently?

If you were the police chief how would you reduce the violence?

What is the difference between a sperm donor and a daddy?

What is the difference between a ghetto and affluent suburb? Why?

How do foreigners make more money in the ghetto than Blacks?

Do you believe in the American dream? What is it?

Do you believe education and hard work pays off?

What are the 3 best ways to become rich in America?

Read and study business plans. What is rule 72 concerning investments?

Some Black males sell crack and some White males sell Cisco. Why?

What is the difference between income and wealth?

What is the median wealth for Blacks and Whites?

Why do more poor people play the lottery?

Why do so many athletes and lottery winners become broke?

"WRITING" for Urban Survival

What would you do differently if you won millions?
Why do some Blacks fight over turf and some
Whites flip turf? What is the difference?

What percent of African Americans vote in your city
for local elections?

"READING" for Urban Survival

Are there more Whites or Blacks below the poverty line?

Do you like positive rap? Name 5 positive rappers? Do you like gangsta rap, why? Name 5 gangsta rappers.

"WRITING" for Urban Survival

Why do radio stations play more gangsta rap? Write and compare the lyrics of a gangsta rapper to Common and Lacrae.

Does gangsta rap create the violence or reflect the current conditions?

What companies control the music industry?

"READING" for Urban Survival

How much do rappers make?

Is it music or musick? What's the difference?

If.... around with 2 b........ but I never make hoes my

misses.....

Whose lyrics are these?

What is the rapper trying to teach you?

What does your choice of music tell about what you value?

Rappers use lyrics describing the way things are but when you look in the mirror, if you don't like what you see, do you change it? Rappers need to have lyrics describing the way they want things to be not the way things are.

Why did 50 Cent file for bankruptcy?

Why do many athletes file bankruptcy soon after they retire?

How much do drug dealers make per day? Per year? Lifetime?

How much do teachers make per day? Per year? Lifetime?

"WRITING" for Urban Survival

Why are so many Black girls pregnant?

Why does 60% of teen pregnancy occur between young girls and older males?

What are your thoughts about child support?

Why does it mean you don't have sex with a person, but all their sexual relations?

What percentage of income does the non-custodial

parent pay in child support?

What percent would a father pay with 5 children

from 5 different mothers?

"WRITING" for Urban Survival

How do you control your anger?

What would make you fight?

Have you experienced racism? Describe.

What is the difference between racism and

prejudice?

"READING" for Urban Survival

How many prisons are in your state?

Are there more Black males in prison or college?

Did you know nationwide, there are more Black men in college than prison?

Why do Black females have a higher high school and college graduation rate than Black males?

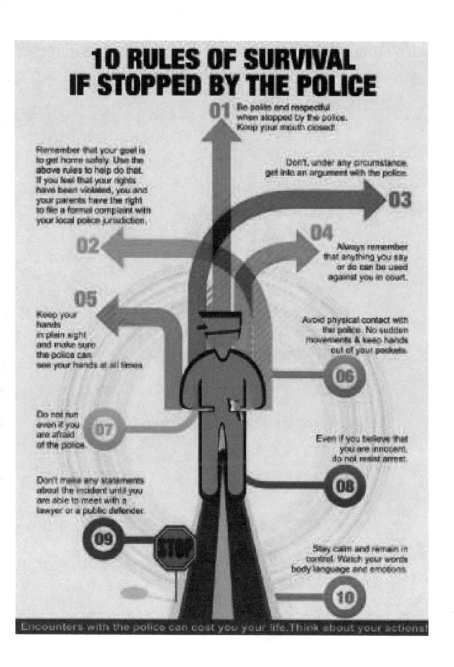

How many Black men are in 4 year public colleges?

Why are so many Black men in jail?

Compare prison to slavery. What are the similarities and differences? How many inmates have lost the right to vote in this democratic country?

Why do so many Blacks die of heart disease, cancer, high blood pressure and diabetes?

"READING" for Urban Survival

Why is AIDS and HIV rampant in prison?

Which drug killed the most people nicotine or crack?

What do you like about school? Dislike?

Who was your favorite teacher? Who is your

favorite teacher? Why?

"READING" for Urban Survival

Who was your "least" favorite teacher? Why?

Why are there so many abandoned houses in the

Black community?

What is your solution to overcome poverty?

What are your feelings about politicians?

How does peer pressure affect you?

"READING" for Urban Survival

Who is your best friend? Why?

Are they honor roll students?

"WRITING" for Urban Survival

If you want to see your future look at your friends.

Are Whites and Asians smarter than Blacks and Hispanics?

Are you better in sports or science? Music or math? Reading or rap?

If no, why not?

What was your favorite book? Why?

Have you ever read a book that you enjoyed so much you could not put it down?

What is good hair?

Is long hair better than short hair?

Are light skin people better looking than dark skin people?

How did we get light-skinned African Americans?

What is the one drop blood theory?

How many African Americans are "passing" for White?

Have you ever seen a rap video with dark skin females fully dressed with short hair? Why not?

What are four benefits of dark skin?

Why do some Whites spend hours trying to get a tan?

Why do some Blacks shy away from the sun to avoid becoming darker?

Describe a mama's boy.

When does a boy become a man?

Have you ever been bullied?

"READING" for Urban Survival

What are your thoughts about snitching?

When does a girl become a woman?

How do you avoid a fight?

How do you avoid being shot?

Describe your thoughts about Africa and Black history.

What is the Olmec civilization?

"WRITING" for Urban Survival

Did Africans arrive in America before Columbus?

Did Columbus really discover America? Why is Columbus Day a holiday?

"READING" for Urban Survival

What is a discovery? Was Columbus the first person in America?

Who is the father of medicine Imhotep or Hippocrates?

Who was Marcus Garvey and Ella Baker?

"WRITING" for Urban Survival

Who built the first pyramids Romans, Greeks or

Africans?

What year were they built?

"READING" for Urban Survival

What percent of Whites during slavery owned slaves? What was the position of Whites during slavery who did not own slaves?

What are the parallels between slavery and the holocaust?

"WRITING" for Urban Survival

What are the similarities between Emmett Till in
1955 and Tamir Rice in 2014?

How many Africans died in America during slavery?
Why do some states no longer use the word slavery
in their textbook?

"READING" for Urban Survival

What was Black Wall Street?

Why do some schools take Egypt out of Africa and

place it in the Middle East?

Did you know Black people from Egypt built the

pyramids and the first civilization?

Did you know Frederick Douglass was beat during slavery attempting to read?

Why was a Black girl suspended when she showed a parallel between the challenges Douglass faced trying to read and Blacks today having the same difficulty?

"READING" for Urban Survival

What do you know about Malcolm X? Please read his autobiography. Why did Malcolm not return to prison? Did you know, he read the dictionary cover to cover?

Malcolm understood the power of reading. Do you?

"WRITING" for Urban Survival

Why do some schools Whitewash slavery?

Some schools and textbooks replace the word slaves with immigrants or workers. What are your thoughts?

What is the difference between the words immigrants and workers?

What is the difference between indentured servant and slave?

"WRITING" for Urban Survival

Why does the Jewish community remind themselves regularly that 6 million Jews died in the Holocaust?

How many Africans died in America during slavery?

"READING" for Urban Survival

Why do Jews use the phrase, "Never Forget"?

What can Blacks learn from the Jewish community?

Did your history begin on a plantation in 1620 or on pyramids 2780 B.C.?

If Blacks are inferior why do some Whites discriminate?

"READING" for Urban Survival

Two male teens are drag racing in a residential neighborhood. They hit a car with both parents and 3 children, the parents are killed and the children survive. One teen is paralyzed for life and the other teen is indicted for involuntary manslaughter and given a life sentence. What did you learn from the above?

Why is it when a White person kills multiple people they are viewed as an individual, who needs mental treatment? But, when a Black person commits a similar crime, the entire race is judged. They view the Black person as a subhuman or animal who deserves the death penalty.

"WRITING" for Urban Survival

What is the leading killer in the Black community? Homicide or abortion? There are 13 homicides daily.

Did you know almost 1,800 Black babies are aborted daily? What are your feelings about abortion?

Is abortion the new form of birth control?

Why are STDs and AIDS higher in the Black community than any other group?

How can the Black community be so violent with 85,000 churches?

What are the lyrics trying to convey in, "Can't Leave Him Alone" by Ciara and 50?

Do females give more play to scholars, ballers or thugs?

"READING" for Urban Survival

Why do some Black females fight?

Why do some Black females fight over boys?

"WRITING" for Urban Survival

Are some Black females loud?

Do some Black females have an attitude?

Is it better to have 5 mates or one?

Can a mother keep a male teenager in the house evenings, weekends and summers trying to keep her son safe?

"READING" for Urban Survival

Have you ever been depressed? Suicidal?

What makes you depressed?

What challenges do you have with your friends?

Parents? Teachers?

"WRITING" for Urban Survival

Write your biography.

Write your resume.

Write your obituary.

"READING" for Urban Survival

Do you have a temper and anger problem? How do you control it?

If you eat 3 meals a day for a week, but only eliminated 3 in a week where are the other 18 meals?

How can educators in Atlanta who changed test scores receive greater punishment than Wall Street embezzlers?

What is wrong with using, "you is"? What is the difference between than and then, there and their, affect and effect, advise and advice, compliment and complement, desert and dessert, loss and lost, worse and worst, later and latter, and further and farther?

How are African Americans 12% of the population, but 50% of foster care?

"READING" for Urban Survival

Do you think your gang members would change your underwear and feed you if you were paralyzed?

Which day is more popular Mother's Day or Father's Day? Why?

What are your thoughts about an ex-boyfriend killing his ex-girlfriend and children because she wants to be with someone else?

"WRITING" for Urban Survival

What is the difference between a male, boy and man?

What is the difference between a female, girl and woman?

Should people marry or shack? What are the advantages and disadvantages?

What is the Willie Lynch syndrome? Give current examples and illustrations.

"READING" for Urban Survival

Has racism changed from 1816? 1916? 2016?

What is the difference between Jim Crow and James Crow Esquire?

How important is a mentor? Do you have one?

Do some mothers raise their daughters and love their sons? What are the consequences?

"WRITING" for Urban Survival

Are females more responsible and mature?

Watch the movie *Fruitvale Station.* What did you learn about Oscar Grant?

What are your favorite YouTube videos?

Why are there more currency exchanges, loan and pawn shops than banks in poor neighborhoods?

"READING" for Urban Survival

Why do credit card companies give them to unemployed teens?

Why do credit card companies encourage you to pay the minimum?

What is a credit score? What is the range?

What are the implications of a credit score?

"WRITING" for Urban Survival

What is a budget?

Design a budget making minimum wage at $16,000 and college degree at $50,000.

Design a budget for yourself.

What are your thoughts about the statement: Poor people spend, middle class people save and rich people invest?

"READING" for Urban Survival

What is the difference between a consumer, saver and investor?

Why was a teacher fired teaching her students about the New York Central Park Five?

What was the case about?

"WRITING" for Urban Survival

A father drops his freshman off to school. The father returns home to take a nap before going to work. His son ditches school and sneaks home and enters through a basement window. The father thought he was a burglar and fatally shoots him.

Your thoughts?

How much money do Black Americans earn?

What percent do they spend with Black businesses?

"READING" for Urban Survival

How does this affect Black unemployment?
What percent of White income is spent with Black businesses?

What percent of the students in your school district are African American?

What percent of the school budget goes to Black businesses?

What percent of the students are White?

What percent of the school budget goes to White businesses?

What percent of the city is Black? White?

What percent of the city budget goes to Blacks? Whites?

If America believes in democracy, why don't they make it easier to register and vote?

"READING" for Urban Survival

How do you feel about every high school graduate receiving a voter registration card with their diploma?

Why are some states trying to suppress voting?

How many Black men are incarcerated in your state?

Why does the media try to convince you, there are more Black males in prison than college?

Did the media exclude Black men in private and 2 year colleges?

How many Black men are in 4 year colleges?

Do Blacks expect schools and the government to raise their children?

What is reparations?

"READING" for Urban Survival

Did America pay reparations to Asians? Native Americans?

What does America owe five million plus African Americans for 246 years working 12 hours, 6 days per week, plus penalty and interest?

What is the quality of most streets named after Martin Luther King?

How would he feel if he walked down those streets?

"WRITING" for Urban Survival

What are the advantages and disadvantages attending a Historical Black College or University?

What do you know about the atrocity to Black people in Tuskegee, Tulsa, New Orleans and Flint?

How are public schools funded?

Is it fair to all students?

"READING" for Urban Survival

How do some students have an advantage on the ACT and SAT?

What do you know about Black fraternities and sororities?

What is hazing? Will you pledge?

What do you know about the criminal justice bail system?

"WRITING" for Urban Survival

Did you know there are people who have been accused of non-violent crimes and are waiting in jail because they cannot afford bail?

If you were in authority, how would you improve the bail system?

What do you know about Khalief Browder? He was a 16 year-old high school student. He was falsely accused of a robbery. Bail was set at $35,000 and his parents could not pay $3500. He was placed in an adult prison. It was one of the most violent in the country. He was beaten by guards and inmates. He spent half his time in solitary confinement. He was released after 3 years. He was traumatized and suicidal. Khalief committed suicide at the age of 22. Please write about all the things wrong about this story and what you will do to prevent it from happening again.

Why is bail 35% higher for Blacks than Whites?

How does excessive bail affect the number incarcerated and how long they stay?

"WRITING" for Urban Survival

Which person would an employer hire? A Black male in a suit with traditional haircut or a Black male with sagging blue jeans, tee shirt, tattoos, with a blonde Mohawk haircut?

What is affirmative action?

Why are so many African Americans between the ages of 18-25 unemployed and out of school?

What are your solutions to solve this problem?

"READING" for Urban Survival

The people in power tell poor people and people of color to get a good education to secure a good job. They tell their children to get a good education and start a business. Which one do you want? A good job or a good business?

Do some schools use special education, gifted and talented, honors, advanced placement and magnet programs as the new form of racial segregation?

How does society discriminate based on zip codes?

What does sex require? Consent.

"WRITING" for Urban Survival

What is sex without consent? Rape.

Have you ever been raped?

Have you ever raped someone?

Have you been a victim of a train?

Have you run a train on someone?

"READING" for Urban Survival

What does it mean the major deterrent to prison is Black men need some respect?

What is the leading killer in the Black community? Police brutality? Cancer? Drug abuse? Heart disease? Suicide? Car accidents? AIDS? Homicides? Abortions? Provide numbers for each.

Has your education taught you to empower or escape your community?

"WRITING" for Urban Survival

How can the Black community improve if its best minds do not live, volunteer, shop, work, or invest in it?

Violence is Black students going to school 12 years and graduating illiterate.

How do you feel about an inmate serving their time, but upon release, their criminal record prevents them from voting, employment and housing?

"READING" for Urban Survival

What is expungement?
Did you know colleges are businesses? You pay them with the expectation, when you graduate, you will secure employment.

Name a different career for each letter of the alphabet excluding sports and entertainment. Research each career.

Majoring in S.T.E.M. Careers will pay annually on average $75,000. Majoring in social science careers will average $35,000. You must earn enough to pay all your expenses, including student loans.

Do you think you got over when they passed you into high school with less than 6th grade test scores?

"WRITING" for Urban Survival

Do you think you got over when they let you graduate from high school with 8th grade test scores?

Which teacher really likes you? The one who allows you to turn in inferior work and receive a passing grade or the one who demands your best and will fail you for anything less?

Did you know colleges will accept you with poor test scores, but make you pay hundreds of dollars for remedial classes that do not receive college credit?

"READING" for Urban Survival

How do you feel about saggin pants? Where did it originate? What are your thoughts about schools that will suspend you over saggin pants? What are your thoughts about cities that will fine you and give jail time over saggin pants? What does saggin spell backwards?

What is your price? How much would I have to pay you to do whatever I want including killing someone?

What is Black Lives Matter? What are the differences and similarities between them and the Civil Rights movement? Does Black Lives Matter negate White Lives Matter?

What are the benefits of voting? How does voting affect jury selection, Pell grants, student loans, school funding, drug laws, judges, police brutality, summer jobs, bail, driving privileges, prison sentences, curfew and truancy? Can you name other issues that politics can affect you?

How does the NBA and NFL help their weaker teams? What can schools and society learn from them?

What are your thoughts about some school districts grading parents on monitoring homework and attending parent meetings? What are your thoughts about some schools and cities fining parents and requiring jail time for tardiness and truancy? What are your thoughts about welfare recipients being required to pass a drug test in order to receive welfare and public housing? Should the middle and upper class also be required in order to receive tax exemptions?

"WRITING" for Urban Survival

Why do so many poor people have parking and driving tickets? Why do so many of them have boots on their cars? Does the city rely on this as a source of income? How can a city be in financial straits, yet pay millions of dollars in police brutality cases? Are there any financial consequences to the police department or officers?

Who is responsible for your health? You or your doctor? Why are there so many cases of sickness, disease and death in the Black community? What causes cancer, heart disease, diabetes and high blood pressure? How available are fruits and vegetables in your neighborhood? How available are fried food restaurants and liquor stores? What does the phrase mean, "You will kill yourself with your knife and fork?" What percent of your body is water? How much water do you drink daily? Many elders who have lived over 90 live by the mantra, eat for nutrition. What are your thoughts?

"READING" for Urban Survival

What is a food dessert?

What percent of civil rights cases against police brutality are decided against the police?

Why do some neighborhoods look better than others? What is redlining? How does it affect insurance and mortgage rates, business loans and city services?

I want you to watch the television show, For My Man. Why would some women do anything for their man? Why would some women steal, distribute and possess drugs, commit fraud and forgery and kill for their man? Do some females have low self-esteem? Do they have male-esteem? Do some value more what he thinks of them then they think of themselves?

Are you addicted to your device? Which gives you the most information? A tweet? Facebook post? News byte? An extensive article? Which do you read the most? How many times daily do you use your mobile device? The average youth looks over 100 times. Could you go a day without it?

How does social media contribute to school violence? Gang violence? How does recording a fight and uploading it contribute to violence? Are most people more interested in taping a fight than breaking it up?

How do you feel about state exams? Do you give your best effort on the exams?

A Black 17-year-old male teenager was dating a White 16-year-old female teenager. She texted him her nude photo and he did not send it to anyone. He was charged with distributing pornography. Your thoughts?

"WRITING" for Urban Survival

Do you want to be great? I have studied great people? They have *six* major habits. What are they?

Great people have *(1) images, pictures and a vision* of what they are trying to achieve. There are people living in ghettos who have never visited downtown and other areas. I encourage you to visit affluent neighborhoods, five star restaurants and hotels, top ranked colleges, airports and read magazines about the rich and famous. You can only go as far as you can see. You must see it before you achieve it. Great people *(2) work hard.* They realize they must develop their talents. Wil Smith said," I am not the most talented, but no one will work harder. If we get on the treadmill together, there are only two options. Either, you will get off first or I am going to die."

"READING" for Urban Survival

They use their *(3) time wisely.* Do you study more than you play video games, watch television, social media, listen to music and surf the Internet? How do you use your time? Create a week chart of how you spent your time. They are *(4) very selective with their choice of friends.* They run with great people. They have a *(5) positive attitude.* They do not use or accept the word can't. They do not accept no for an answer. They have *(6) goals.* What is your goal for this year? Five years? 10 years? 20 years? What is the difference between a goal and a plan?

"WRITING" for Urban Survival

Final Exam for Scholars Only!

America has 5% of the world's population, but 25% of the prison population. America incarcerates 3 million. Japan has 47,000 and Sweden 4,000. America has 15,000 homicides annually. Japan has 395 and Sweden less than 100. The American recidivism is 85% compared to Japan and Sweden's 40%. What can America's criminal justice system learn from Japan and Sweden? What are your thoughts?

"READING" for Urban Survival

In 1920, 90% of Black youth had their fathers at home. In 1980, it was 80%. What is it today? Why? What is the impact of fatherlessness on the Black family?

What are the similarities between racism, sexism and classism? What was Brown vs. Topeka? What are the benefits and problems with this decision?

Is Du Bois' talented tenth committed to empower the 90% or do they look out for themselves?

"WRITING" for Urban Survival

Invictus
By William Ernest Henley

Out of the night that covers me,

Black as the pit from pole to pole,

I thank whatever gods may be

For my unconquerable soul.

In the fell clutch of circumstance

I have not winced nor cried aloud.

Under the bludgeonings of chance

My head is bloody, but unbowed.

Beyond this place of wrath and tears

Looms but the Horror of the shade,

And yet the menace of the years

Finds and shall find me unafraid.

"READING" for Urban Survival

It matters not how strait the gate,

How charged with punishments the scroll,

I am the master of my fate,

I am the captain of my soul.